Heart Like Leaves

Poems by

Barbara Novack

SAN FRANCISCO · FAIRFIELD · DELHI

Heart Like Leaves

Copyright ©2022 by Barbara Novack

All rights reserved. Printed in the United States of America. No part of this book may be used or reproduced in any manner whatsoever without written permission except in the case of brief quotations embodied in critical articles and reviews. For information contact:

1st World Library
PO Box 2211
Fairfield, IA 52556
www.1stworldpublishing.com

Book & Cover Design
Melanie Gendron
melaniegendron999@gmail.com

Cover Photo
Barbara Novack

Author Photo
S. Rita J. Vanson, CIJ

First Edition

ISBN: 978-1-4218-3720-8

Library of Congress Cataloging-in-Publication Data

To Dr. Samir Raby, Hazel Miller, and Colette Martin

for caring, above and beyond.

I am eternally grateful.

With gratitude to

Lloyd Abrams, S. Alice Byrnes, Kathleen and Richard Conway, Michele DeLouise, Joyce DiPinto, Anne and Roger Dupré, Sharon Esposito, Elvira Fedoroff, Roxanne Jacoby, Bob Kinpoitner, Larry and Irene McCoy, Kathy Maher, Alan Marks, Debby Nagler, Trisha O'Neill, Georgina Sculco, Doreen Spungin, Sue Sternberg, Richard Torres, Jr., Fred Velde, Julie Zeidman

special thanks to Diane Frank

candles in the darkness

Holy Acts

*When I bleed my sorrows and concerns
you wipe the red from my lips, my chin
with compassion,
my tears
with your gentle smile,
your words confirming a strength
I don't always feel.
You say it's real.*

*The world turns, these seasons are
the life we live.
Your holy acts are
the gifts you give.*

*When I come with the heat of sorrow and concern
your cool cloth of care and consolation
comforts.*

*A hand reaching out to clasp
in this season of
the life we live,
a holy act,
the gift you give.*

Author's Note

These poems reflect the roller-coaster journey of loss and grieving.

They are best accompanied by a glass of wine or pot of tea and Leonard Cohen's "Hallelujah" played by cello or string quartet.

Ice cream and chocolates are also a possibility and Beethoven's 6th Symphony.

Barbara Novack

The journey . . .

Table of Contents

Dedication iii
Gratitude v
Holy Acts vii
Author's Note ix
Holding Tight 1
The Good Lie 2
Secrets 3
Palimpsest 4
Magical Thinking 6
We talk of cemetery plots 7
Saving Graces 8
The Grand Tour 9
Dark: A Metaphor for This Particular Time 10
I Am Afraid to Go to Sleep 11
ER 12
ICU 13
Inevitable 15
Transition to the Disappear 16
Vigil 17
What Does He Dream? 18
His Dream 19
I need to remember 20
Making It Real 21
Actively Dying 22
Fog 24

There is Nothing Left to Do	25
Center of Attention	26
The world does not end	27
Losing Time	28
Remembering Who I Am	29
Asters	31
Filling the Void	32
Falling Apart	33
How to Get Somewhere	34
The Length of Grief	35
Loss After Loss	36
I Can	38
The Fear	39
I dreamt of my mother last night	41
This Year	42
Sharing Sunset	43
Expectation	44
Heart Like Leaves	46
Photo (Joel Novack)	47
Recoup Bouquet	49
"What we call the beginning…" – T.S. Eliot	51
Acknowledgments	53
About the Author	55

Holding Tight

I was holding so tight to the steering wheel
trying to keep our car on track
while the track inevitably
ended in a ditch.
I climbed out, bruised
soul-battered
weary and worn.
He remained,
to rise
like smoke
and dissipate.
The soot fell on me.

I held on, knuckles white,
hands cramped, gripping air.
I need to let go
but I am frozen in this pose,
clenched, gripping
air.

The Good Lie

Fear and anxiety is what kills
more than disease that
silently erodes. Oh,
there is the pain, but
it can be otherwise explained,
brushed away, slid under
the carpet, covered with
puffs of positivity, pixie dust,
guided by misdirection.
Am I depriving him of
time spent carefully
like scarce gold coin
rather than squandered
like poor pennies, carelessly
tossed away?
I don't know the answer
to the goodness
of the lie.

Secrets

I kept secrets,
held in the toxic truth,
for him
to sustain him
protecting him like a sheepdog
from the wolves
and I herded the doctors too
into the fold
so the howls in the hills
would be faint, in the distance
vague on the night air
floating away like clouds
across the moon.

He didn't want to know.

And then, a year in,
he sat on the examining table
and asked.
Remission?
No.
Terminal?
Yes.

And now he knew.
But still
I knew more.

Palimpsest
for Joel

How old could I have been? Two?
Looking at a photo of my brother when he was not much older.
Sitting on my father's lap as he held the photo album,
I could not explain my tears. I
didn't have the words.
In the photo he
had his face scrunched with the effort of
turning a spigot handle that wouldn't turn.
It was in a park somewhere. The spigot handle wouldn't turn
and he
was trying so hard.
I cried and couldn't stop. My father
didn't know why. Then he realized it was the photo,
the struggle,
that disturbed me so,
and he laughed, saying
it was posed, that he'd told my brother to pretend to turn it,
to show all the effort,
when they both knew it couldn't be turned.

What it was, though, was more than just the photo:
It was the connection I felt
before I had the words, a connection
that was real
that was an "us"
before we were "we."

I felt then what I know now
the palimpsest of our lives
that ever intersection of us.
We knew each other before.

I loved him even before I was born
and he welcomed me
with that same familiarity.

Magical Thinking

I wished him pain
not much, just a little,
because he was so unsympathetic
to mine,
so he could feel it, just a little
and know, to know
just a little.
And then
a diagnosis to dread,
pain, a lot of pain,
and an end
sooner than we'd planned.
And I cry,
and I fear I
wished it on him,
caused it, even
just a little,
and I wish
I could wish it
away.

We talk of cemetery plots

We talk of cemetery plots
ponder pre-planning
reality closer than we'd like
while a blind brain still dreams.
Which is the reality,
the truth in the moment, this
moment
not that one, the one that brackets
time
contains, compresses
heightens it into stone
carves it with etching-acid rain
tears maybe, but we won't see
or know, since
no one's left to tell our story
but the stone
or the cloud-fluff sunbeam-streaked
morning out the kitchen window
where birds peck the spring lawn seeds
and branches bubble with nascent leaves' green haze?
We talk of cemetery plots
ponder pre-planning
wipe condensation from our eyes
with an index finger
draw a smiley face on the hazed window pane
where we can, if we dare,
look out and see
tomorrow.

Saving Graces

Sliding into summer
oblivious but not
time moving quickly
but not
the day to day filled
with impending loss
as he disappears
in front of me
the day to day filled
with saving graces
as I remember to embrace
colors and light
green and red and pink
grass and leaves
roses and azalea
and sunshine
golden and warm
countering the chill
sere, barren terrain
to come.

Nature is nature
a purity I can
lose myself in
a beauty that sustains
as spring's brief burgeoning
blossoms bright into summer.
I savor
savor still
savor always
knowing fall and winter come
with their own
saving graces.

The Grand Tour

Three hospitals locally
and we've seen them all
not in passing on the road
on the way to fun
but from emergency room triage
to curtained cell
and too often the rooms so similar
place to place
their neutral colors and brown-gray floors blur.
We've seen them all
as his illness phases
into the weaknesses it creates
bubbling into his lungs,
heating his body,
and fissuring his bones.
The Grand Tour used to be
an occasion for wonder
visiting the glories of unfamiliar places.
We are visiting the unknown
in too-familiar places
and the wonder is
I always take him home.

Dark: A Metaphor for This Particular Time

light is gone
can't find the chime
to meditate on
no ohm
of centering calm

light brings joy
choice in abundance
waiting for me
to open the door
to happy

but there is no light
no choice, no chime
just dark
a metaphor
for this particular
time.

I Am Afraid to Go to Sleep

I am afraid to go to sleep
strange new pattern I analyze
to find the why.
I am afraid to go to sleep
not because I am afraid I'll die, but
because I will wake up
in another day
too much like this one
only further along;
the "stop" of it is happening
(not my doing)
will end all the universes I know
(out of my control)
but the smallest, the one left behind.

I am afraid to go to sleep
to learn the next day's lessons
ahead of time
in dreams that really don't come because I don't sleep
won't sleep, can't sleep.
I try to ease around the edges of
moving on
when the place it goes is not where I want it to
by watching movies all night
to stop the maybe-drowse
that might take me into
the real tomorrow,
not like the nighttime thought of
but the real one
of discussions and instructions and sadness
and keeping a happy face
the real tomorrow that ends in the brick wall of forever.
Each day wanes on the cusp of responsibility
the weight of knowledge
and I am afraid to go to sleep.

ER

They work to get his fever down,
his blood pressure up.
Prognosis: Dire.
They work. I watch.
They work. I wait
holding the bag with his belongings
that will go home, I am sure
without him.

I wait
for the inevitable
that I knew was coming
but hoped would not come
so soon.

In this antiseptic beeping environment
chill with the hollow wind of fear
of knowing the unknown
now so close
I touch its curtain,
feel the weave of the fabric
not so gossamer after all
more shroud-like.

What's to be done
but remain
as long as the road rises.
After that
they say
there is stillness
but sun.

ICU

He is in the ICU,
alive
despite predictions otherwise.
I am grateful.
He craves potato chips
and chocolate chip cookies.
I get bags and bags from the gift shop
happy that he craves
something.
He is cared for attentively
and they are so kind, these nurses,
easing my anxiety
and his.
Whose is greater?
How can we know?
They are about
different emptinesses.

Two days later,
I arrive to an empty bed.
My heart thumps in my ears.
Information, I need information!
Is he . . . ?

No one to ask.
The nurses station deserted.
A familiar aide comes by, pushing a cart.
I ask her.
"What happened? Is he . . . ?"

Her hand goes comforting to my arm.
"They moved him this morning.
He's in a regular room, downstairs."

My heart throbs, my chest burns;
I hurry to the elevator.
He is still here.
He is still alive!

And I am grateful.

Inevitable

It starts slow
this toboggan ride
soft hillocks, only slight inclines,
but gravity pulls
and speed increases
and the denied
makes the hills higher
and increases the slide.

It starts slow
and there are curves
and twists
but then
it becomes
a straight straight ride
and we hold on
to each other
as long as we can
until it is just I
my arms around your waist
my face in the warmth of your back
with a memory of
holding on.

Transition to the Disappear

They go somewhere
and then somewhere else
on their way
to the never return
distances
increasing distances
to make the separation
of apart
of gone
in stages
of disappear.

Vigil

He will go when he's ready to go.
He will know, decide.
It is not up to me,
I can't keep him here
much as I might want to.
My vigil is for me
to be with him
the breathing him
however hard those breaths might become.
He won't know
not really.
He may sense but
he may not even be here then;
he may be drifting
testing out the clouds.
The vigil is for me
for us to be we
a while longer.

What Does He Dream?

What does he dream in his stupored slumber,
the illness sucking him into constant sleep?
I watch the breaths, the chest rising, shallower and shallower,
the mouth gaping, dark,
the face unshaven these weeks
as never before, he
so assiduous about such things.
Is such sleep dreamless
or is he navigating a new terrain,
viewing brochure images
through the partly opened door?
No expression on his face of savoring beauty
just perhaps a vague interest
as if still deciding if this is a trip
he wants to take.
He will have no choice, though want
may be a factor, will another,
wanting it, willing it, pushing to the threshold
or pushing it away.
Or is it just a sleep, deep, dark
mysterious as life itself
or death
which, of course, is what
we are talking about,
death peering too closely
watching as I am
knowing what I do not
for Death sits much closer now
than I.

His Dream

He said he was dreaming of being well again
of getting out of bed and walking around
getting himself washed and dressed
shaved, hair combed, teeth brushed
all the things
he cannot do
now
or ever again.
"I've never been this sick," he says.
"Why do I feel this way?
Why is my voice so weak?
It's harder and harder
to communicate."
He says it in barely audible whispers,
face gaunt and unshaven, hair matted
cannula in his nose, IV in his side,
lying small in a bed,
dreaming big.

I need to remember

I need to remember
the before time
before the sadness
the time of laughter, banter
but the after time
is pervasive
the narrowing hallway
length perhaps predetermined
end definitely
that door that opens
on silent hinges
that door you don't even have to push
that door that awaits
us all
but
for you (and for me)
its presence loomed
with imminence.
Now the door is opening
the hallway narrowed
shoulder wide
for you
and I watch you go
trying to remember
before.

Making It Real

I'm writing poems to make it real
what I'm seeing, what I'm feeling
what I know to be true
but
don't want to see, feel or know.
What I can't make go away
I write about to see, feel, know, again still,
not to torture myself (I don't think)
but to help make it register somehow, all
that is so painful. I am crumbling inside
just shopping in the supermarket
buying for me not us.
He hasn't accompanied me
even been able to help put the purchases away
in months. I am used to the alone part
but not the alone whole,
and I write the poems to fill
the hole.

Actively Dying

an oxymoron
ends bending away from each other
circling around
to meet
where they shouldn't

He finally had a phone
in the new place
the rehab getting better place
in the emergency-ICU-hospital rooms
I could not talk to him
unless I was there
but in the new getting better place
he had a phone
and I could talk to him without being there
the half of his stay he could talk
and on the Thursday on that phone I heard
the chest rumbles and rattles again
and I called the nurses station
the care center
wherever I could until
I could get a doctor
to check if the pneumonia was back.
"No," the doctor told me,
"no pneumonia, vitals stable,
he's OK."

Then, the next day, Friday,
the doctor called again.
"Get here," he said.
"Vitals unstable. He's actively dying."

And so it began
or ended
or continued to where it was already going
in the place of getting better
and I was there and there and there
as his voice whispered and disappeared
as he slept
and he struggled to breathe
and, on Tuesday,
as he stared at the wall.
I knew it would be that night
but I wasn't there
and it was OK.
It was OK that I wasn't there
because he wasn't either
anymore.
Actively dying simply ends
in dying.

Fog

Gray haze, fine droplets of mist
soft-edged shapes emerge
only with proximity.
It is easy to get lost.
It is easy to collide
with solidity.
It is not easy
to see the way ahead.

I drift like the droplets
hanging on air currents
in a cloud of
gray uncertainty.
Maps are useless.
Light bounces back.
There is no guidance
or path through.

There is just the haze
and the fine droplets
like tears.

There is Nothing Left to Do

There is nothing left to do
except be.
I have made all the arrangements
made all the phone calls
sent all the emails and texts
navigated this initial
labyrinth.
There are more.
I lie in bed
thinking of them
thinking of other things too
remembering
mostly the end times
before that is harder.
It will come, they tell me,
the before time will dominate
eventually
in time
when there is time
to breathe
even though, right now
there is nothing left to do.

Center of Attention

When he left, I
became the center of attention; I
don't want to be anymore. It
was OK for a while, when I
needed handholding, when I
needed the strength of
being surrounded by love. But
now, I
don't feel like checking in
every day, telling them I
still have a pulse, still
am doing things, still
am tired, feel the loss, still . . .
I don't want to be reminded I
am the only one left. I
don't want to be living
in a grave
anymore.

The world does not end

The world does not end
or begin again.
I am not made anew
in this time.
The universe continues
continues
the motes of dust
alter
but do not disappear.
There is a law
a rule
of the universe
a conservation
of energy:
it is all there
forever
just changing.
The world does not end
or begin anew.
I am not made again
just made and remade
of the same star stuff
over and over
again.

Losing Time

I bounce off the world
its surface no longer porous
no longer absorbing me;
it is hard now
plastic smoothly molded
with no handholds
no footholds, no space, no place
to grab onto, I
collide and careen
into the darkness
space place emptiness
the crumbling
held within by the shell
that's harder, that cracks
but doesn't shatter.
I lose time
spend, waste time
on the unnecessary,
chipping, snipping, clipping the edges
while the center stays undone.
Losing time, losing I'm:
I am not, any longer, me

Remembering Who I Am

I was him for so long
I realize it now.
"You love me too much," he'd say.
"I don't know how to love you
any other way,"
I'd reply.
I kept a corner of my life, perhaps,
my poems, my books
but the rest
was him
and there was no rest
just running, caring,
phone calls and medications
and concern
and late night tears
and watching him disappear
thinner and thinner
clothes sagging
face hollow
arms sticks
ribs and vertebrae
countable.
And the emergency rooms
and hospital rooms
punctuating the daily doctor visits.
It was he, his life, his journey.
It became me, my life,
my journey
for we had always
been we
we two.
Now me.
Now me

just me.
In the vast desert
dry, parched sunbaked days
chill, empty nights
my silent screams echo
until
like lost puzzle pieces
like the Scrabble game
with a missing letter
I find, hidden
beneath couch cushions
in the dusty unswept corners
of the empty rooms
in the pockets of jackets
he will never wear again
pieces of what was
that can make me whole
like old photographs
that remind me
who I was
who I am.

Asters

They appear in my backyard
among the already there
asters, yellow hearts and purple petals
reaching arms among
the already bloomed green.
They appear like hope, like consolation
after the great loss
beauty
on this sunny October day
with blue sky and fluffy clouds
so perfect
among life's imperfection
a thank you
from him to me,
he who never noticed such things
but notices them now,
from the bigger him
who provides such things,
or, without my assistance,
from me to both
in gratitude.

Filling the Void

I am trying to fill the void
but I am always empty
food does not fill me
does not satisfy
the supermarket purchases –
too many; I am only
shopping for one now –
do not satisfy
rather unnerve
as I fill shelves
with too many cans
too many jars
food that will not fill me
will not satisfy
fill the refrigerator
with too much fruit
too many vegetables
perishables that will rot
if I don't consume
what does not fill me
what does not satisfy.

I am only filling space
I cannot fill the void.

Falling Apart

I am flying apart
my big bang
from the dense core of
holding it together
doing all the needed-to-be-done
to
can't get anything done.
I am flying apart
the center isn't holding
falling apart.

How to Get Somewhere

Thinking of how to get somewhere
he used to drive to
for business I have to take care of
for him
I say (to myself
no one else here anymore),
"I'll find my way,"
meaning, of course, I'll
find directions, I'll
Google, but
"I'll find my way"
resonates
as an answer
to the pain.

The Length of Grief

Grief is long
and wide
and meanders
like the Mississippi
and like the Mississippi
it starts far
from its end
a trickle in the unknown reaches
to a gush into the tributary
to a rolling flow in the river
to a spewing end
as its mouth spits
into the unending vastness.
But perhaps we are not so propelled
to the end
into the vastness
his and mine
different, but
similar
his beyond a veil
a door with no knob
mine in place
on an unsettled surface.
When grieving is long
grief
is a cup of tea
a chocolate bar
a piece of pizza
lunch with our friends
the nightly phone call with mine;
grief is
floating on the river
that started
far from its end.

Loss after Loss

They are packing their bags
mentally now,
physically in six weeks.
They are leaving
ending our years
together
emptying the shelves
boarding up the windows
turning out the lights
locking the door
taking down his shingle.
They have closed their eyes
turned their back
on the past
and I understand:
when you start asking
"Is this all there is?"
it is time for more
time to move on
time for positive change.
I understand.
But my world has already
shifted seismically this year
the fates kicking out the legs
of the stool I stand on
to see beyond;
now I see only here
drilled into the hole
of the moment
and now they are taking away
the last of stability
the pillar I clung to
as, in the quaking world,

the tsunami pulled at me.
It swept him away
as I tried to hold on
to him I could not
to their pillar I did
and now they are taking it
away.

I sink to the weeping depths
of loss
after loss.

I Can

I can eat ice cream
from the container
peanut butter from the jar
I can double dip
I don't have to share
I can leave the bathroom door open
walk around in my underwear (or less)
I can
I can
I can
I am alone in this space now
once occupied by four
then three
then two
now just me
I can
I can
but I can't
bring them back.

The Fear

They've all gone away
from this house
to hospitals
and never returned
leaving their lives
in the middle
of life
clothes on the chair
shoes under the bed
to-do lists on the dresser
appointments, plans –
but they never returned.
I was always there
returning,
as three, then two, now one
the backstop to catch
life's remainders,
to fold it all up
pack it away
tie up the loose
dangling ends
tidy up
seal the envelope
of the life.
I was always there.
They could look behind them
and know
the crumpled tissues
would be thrown away
the half-written letter
would be finished and mailed
the bills would be paid
and the final arrangements
would be made.

But I look behind me
and no one's there.
No one's left
to catch the remainder
to tidy up.

I fear leaving
but more, I fear
not returning.

I dreamt of my mother last night

I dreamt of my mother last night;
she's gone 7 1/2 years now.
I dream of her,
I see her in shadows even awake.
She stands around corners
just out of reach.
When I dream of her,
I always remember, but
last night's dream
has stayed with me differently,
well into the day.
She'd left pie, pieces of pie
in the refrigerator
like she did after her luncheons
with the seniors,
the holiday leftovers
that I'd eat for breakfast.
She left pie for me
and I looked for her, wondering
where she was.
"Where's Mom?" I called
to my brother,
but he was gone
too.
I dreamt of my mother last night
and I guess my brother too.
I dreamt of a gift of pie
and an empty house.

This Year

This year
all is changed.
I thought
the ones before
had difficulties
but we were two
then;
I could lean
and not fall
then.
This year
all is changed
"Be strong," I'm told.
Strength is
in the moment
and the ones to come,
resilience,
but the steel core
of family
is gone.
Friends have tensile strength
but
I return
to a dark, silent
house.
Can it still be
home?
This year all
is changed:
I, being,
among ghosts.

Sharing Sunset

Day after Thanksgiving
my first alone
I bustling about the house
tending to cares
that used to be shared
alone
and I pass the kitchen window
the one west facing
and notice the horizon's hint of pink
and I turn to the other kitchen window
the one southwest facing
(I track the seasons between them)
and the frame is filled with glory
streaks of pink and magenta purpling
and I pause,
feeling the warmth around me
and I thank them
those who've left
with whom I shared these moments
before
for sharing with me
now.

Expectation

I read an article
see a TV listing
think, "I have to show this to him,
tell him about this,"
and then I remember.

We used to leave notes for each other
on the kitchen counter.
I'd get up for work before
his retiree wake-up time
and the note would be there
left the night before:
"Have a good day, Barb.
(He was the only one
who called me Barb)
See you later.
Love, Joel"
and I would take that note
put it in my pocketbook
to keep it with me
and then I'd write one for him
saying very much the same thing:
"Have a good day, Joel.
See you later.
Love, B."
I come downstairs in the mornings now
expecting to see his note
but the counter is empty.

I have a cousin
who still expects
to speak to her mother
now gone ten years.

It doesn't go away
the expectation
the thought, "I have to tell him,
he'll want to know,
it will interest him."

It doesn't go away,
does it?

Heart Like Leaves

I stare out the window
at the gray of autumn's end
my heart, like leaves
broken from the stem
from the branch
from the trunk
prey to wind now
to weather now
untethered now,
my heart like leaves.

But even in this bare-branched world
something of our life
survives
as heart-like leaves
prey to wind, to weather
broken from the stem
fall at my doorstep
and I smile
for you are here
still and love-real
in each season's cycle
in each turn
of the wheel.

Recoup Bouquet

*Gather it together
into a bunch like flowers
recoup bouquet*

*Gather it together
the pain
in all its colors
with its own perfume
hold it
know it
its gift is knowledge
and the dark beauty of loss
that is its own grace
the leaving
in its own time
when one must*

*Gather it together
the sand
and the shards
the hourglass broken*

*Gather it together
time that was
time that is*

*Gather it together
recoup bouquet*

What we call the beginning is often the end
And to make an end is to make a beginning.
The end is where we start from.

– T.S. Eliot, "Little Giddings"

Acknowledgments

These poems appeared in the same or similar form in the following publications:

"The Good Lie" in *Nassau County Poet Laureate Society Review* Vol. VIII (2020)

"We talk of cemetery plots" in *Poets Speaking to Poets: Echoes and Tributes*, Eds. Nicholas Fargnoli and Robert Hamblin. ArsOmnia Press, 2021

"Saving Graces" in *The Weekly Avocet* #446 (6/20/21)

"Asters" in *The Weekly Avocet* #463 (10/17/21)

"Vigil" in Long Island Quarterly 2021

"The Length of Grief" in *Nassau County Voices in Verse* 2022, Ed. James Wagner. Local Gems Press, 2022

Cover photo by Barbara Novack

Photo p. 47: Joel Novack by David Marks

Author photo by S. Rita J. Vanson, CIJ

About the Author

Barbara Novack is Writer-in-Residence and member of the English Department at Molloy University. She founded and hosts Poetry Events there and, off-campus, presents highly regarded creative writing programs and workshops. Her books include the novel *J.W. Valentine*, nominated for a Pulitzer Prize and finalist for Pushcart Press Editor's Book Award, full-length poetry collections *Something Like Life*, and *Dancing on the Rim of Light*, and chapbooks *Do Houses Dream?* and *A Certain Slant of Light*, both finalists for the Blue Light Press Poetry Prize.

www.ingramcontent.com/pod-product-compliance
Lightning Source LLC
Chambersburg PA
CBHW032135090426
42743CB00007B/606